What Bends Us Blue

What Bends Us Blue

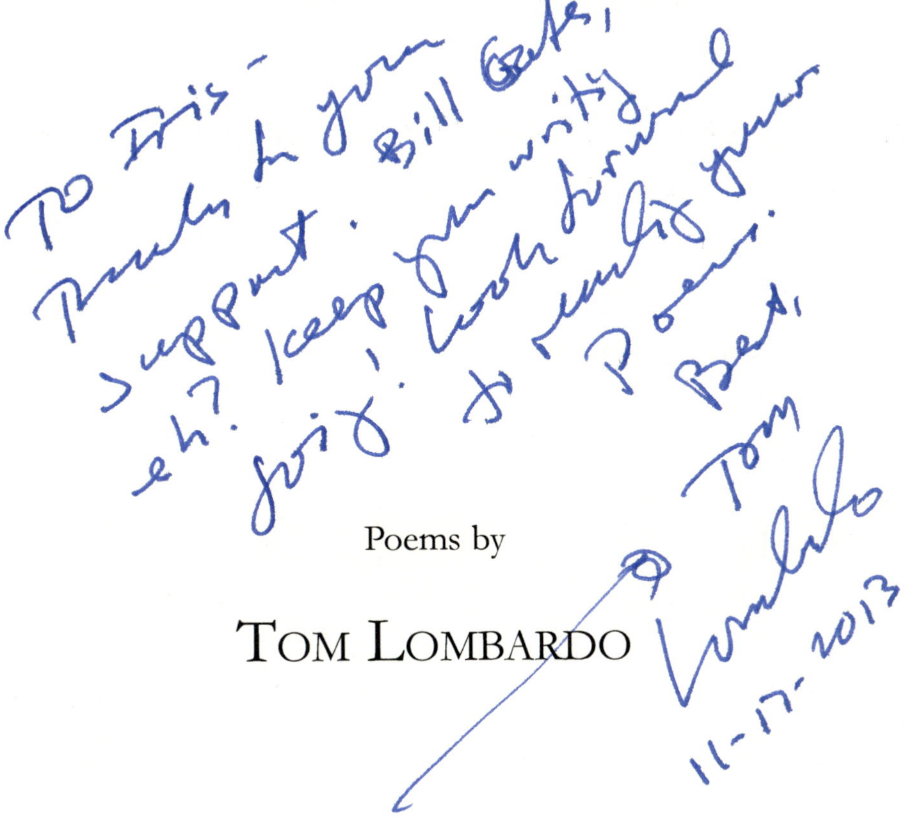

Poems by

TOM LOMBARDO

WordTech Editions
Cincinnati, Ohio

Published by WordTech Editions
P.O. Box 541106
Cincinnati, OH 45254-1106

ISBN: 9781625490247
LCCN: 2013938910

Poetry Editor: Kevin Walzer
Business Editor: Lori Jareo

Visit us on the web at www.wordtechweb.com

For Hope, Lucia, and Sante

Acknowledgments

Thanks to the editors of the following journals in which these poems first appeared.

Ambit (UK) "Smoking Volcano Tops" and "Keys to the Solar System" Fall 2007

Ascent, "The Poet Chooses His Drug" Vol. 29 No. 2 Winter 2005

Chrysalis Reader, "Elegy" Vol. 12 2005 and "Daffodils" Vol. 13 2007

Hampden-Sydney Poetry Review, "*Sanguine Noce*" Winter 2005 and "How Bill Gates Saved My Marriage" Winter 2008

Kritya: A Journal of Poetry (India), "Dense Nodular Opacity" March 2009

Lady Jane's Miscellany, "Games of Chance" Winter 2008/09

Mad Hatter's Review, "The Inventor" Summer 2005

New Millenium Writings, "Sam and Abraham" Winter 2007/08 Honorable Mention

New York Quarterly, "When" No. 61 Fall 2004

Orbis: Quarterly International Literary Review (UK), "Elegy on a Visitation" No. 135 Winter 2005/06

Pearl, a Literary Magazine, "The Minute I Met Lana" No. 37 2007

Poet Lore, "Split Second To Blink" Vol. 99 No. 3/4 Fall/Winter 2004

Pravasi Duniya (India), "Daffodils" Nov. 2010, translated to Hindi by Satyendra Srivastava

Salamander, "Keys to the Solar System" Fall 2007

Southern Poetry Review, "My Little Heart Attack" Vol. 43 No. 1 Spring/Summer 2004

Thanal Online (India), "Dyin' Blues" Fall 2009, translated to Mayalayam by C.P. Aboobacker

What Bends Us Blue

FOREWORD

xi

Blue woolen tie, blue-domed tent, eyes moon blue, copblue jodhpurs, blue arrows on hospital-white linoleum, a surreal yet utterly plausible blue sun: the color code of Tom Lombardo's debut collection, *What Bends Us Blue,* is so deep and wide with feeling it's fair to say the reader plunges into an emotional element that's oceanic. Lombardo's sensibility is comic, Keatonesque in its pratfalls, but he knows what the good comic knows: humor invites pathos but repels bathos. Only a poet alert to this distinction could write such a sonically exuberant poem about anti-depressives. Everywhere we're reminded that one must be positive in the face of loss because loss is a given, as in the gloriously deadpan "My Little Heart Attack," which "went by so fast/it didn't stop my singing." Lombardo turns lost keys into a fabulist, rhapsodic love poem to the foibles that make a marriage a marriage; he handles "death's paperwork" with brave efficiency in a suite of potent elegies; he does so many things poets ought to do that he earns the bardic authority embedded in his name—and our trust.

Steven Cramer
Director
Lesley University MFA Program in Creative Writing
Author, *Clangings* and *Goodbye to the Orchard*

I.

A Grip on the Blues

Bending a note
to resolve the blues requires
a grip by the lips
on the harp's second hole.
Suck a mouth-sized hurricane,
drop your jaw fast and quick
like a sky diver stepping off *WHA*…
while your tongue digs a trough
to your lungs and the *oooo*
boils your blood blue.

The Poet Chooses His Drug

Paxil® starts with a pop,

      unsettling the air, made louder

         by the explosion in its midsection,

            gastrics in excess

              spurt into a tail

      that lingers indefinitely at your tongue-palate interface,

           inducing no confidence in one

who has what I have.

The other SSRIs in my PDR

         —Prozac®—

        the sound frightens children

          into nightmares.

The word spits at you.

      Then, its long *o* like the cry of a vampire

         who snoozes in the wrong place,

          a coffin surrounded

         by prone-axe wielding SS agents:

—Serzone®—

a military salute with clicking heels

and rifles snapping to attention.

Serzone® orders you into well-being

as wide and deep

as its mouth-filling long *o*

and never-ending nasal.

Those two don't sound like they'd help what I have.

Why do they use so many *z*'s in drug names?

And long *o*'s?

I'd heard that pharmaceutical companies hire poets

to invent the names of drugs.

Makes sense—a poet to elevate

a chemical named sertraline

to Zoloft® ,

to hack Prozac®

from fluoxetine hydrochloride,

to erect Viagra®

from sildenafil citrate.

An industry insider invited me to send my resume,

       warning me not to spread the word because,

       you know, poets?

       Inventing drug names?

That's like a honeybee from PETA

           pollinating a Venus fly trap.

Imagine the introduction at a reading:

       "…we are honored to welcome

the Poet Laureate of Pfizer, maker of Viagra®.

       His three-syllable, Latinate creation

           of sound and sens-

uality has been purchased and enjoyed

by 256 million satisfied readers around the world…"

I like the sound of Zoloft® best.

    The softest sibilant eases my larynx

        into the low-tension long *o* vowel,

            which pours nicely through liquid to

                —ah—

        fricative eases into the faintest of plosives,

a soft landing, but a landing no less.

      Zoloft® is Gregory Peck as Atticus Finch,

          who would never have what I have.

The Minute I Met Lana

I met her in Cincinnati,
sitting poolside.
Her bikini,
lime. Hair, flame red.

I dove, came up between her legs,
Have those freckles
all over your
bod? She slid her

shades down her nose, green eyes glared, blinked.
Her accent, *Ah*
assure you, Ah
do! And she did.

Her Constellations

Polaris was her navel.
I always started there,
my kiss and my tongue
tipped her into giggles.

Though Ptolemy, Hevelius, Tycho Brahe
preceded me, I made discoveries here
and there. Using mirrors, we traversed
her universe. We named, renamed.

Andromeda. Lyra. Camelopardalis.
She studied the Northern sky
while I sampled freckles,
red stars in a sky of pink.

Draco. Cygnus. Canis Venetici.
Pegasus. Boötes. Coma Berenices.
My lips' careering caresses lost their way.
She'd remind me, *Don't forget my Lynx.*

She had a bright Corona Borealis,
three degrees north of her clitoris
on the way to her Triangulum.
But we never named a Cancer—

not for its Herculean failures
nor its dimness nor its beehive—
the thought made her squeamish—
across her belly, a giant, clicking crab.

How Bill Gates Saved My Marriage

I.

My wife doesn't know it but I track her cycles
on Microsoft Outlook's calendar function.
Before Outlook, I once said, *Your mother doesn't*—whack!
I'm on the floor looking at the ceiling thinking
Now. What was that about?
Even though I've read about the luteal phase and PMS
in *Esquire*, *Redbook*, WebMD, I was thrown off track
by two pregnancies—cycles disappeared—serenity

yet to see again before her menopause.
It took me years of ceiling analysis
to comprehend cyclic nadirs.
Outlook plans that period each month
when I must agree with every single thing—
Summer trip to Disney World with the kids? By train?

II.

—until I see tampons in the trash.
Outlook's drawback: testy engineers
programmed precisely perfect
28-day cycles. Real-life biology instigates disaster
like the time, a day too late, I said, *Michele Kwan never deserved gold.*
Whack! I'm on the floor again, thinking
I'd better adjust my Outlook.

Yet, with fine-tuning, I've discovered months
go by in matrimonial harmony
thanks to Mr. Gates'
little reminder box that pops up
on the 26th day in menses time—
Egg ready to blow.
Walk tiptoe.

Games of Chance

I toss my cards to the middle. Another loser.
Time to take a piss to change my luck.

I drain my Bushmills, leave the table. From the bathroom,
I hear voices digging down to whispers, snickers,

grunts. Winners gloat. Whiners bloat.
Mike, with a cough, Frank, with a prostate—one day, losers.

Their choice: insert barrel between teeth and spin.
My heart races at the pounding sound of urine.

I'm down to my last few chips. I've lost
enough to cover all expenses

for that trip to Greece with Nan, her checkout
voyage. After biopsy, diagnosis,

a plastic funnel intubates her aorta
between ribs II and III.

She pours in chemo weekly.
HER-2/*neu* oncogene expresses itself

as significant adverse prognosis,
cascading to decreased survival.

I'm with Nan when she decides to stay
in the Cyclades, though her body flies home

the following week. I help bury her in the Mediterranean.
By now, a thousand bubbles yellow the water.

Time to shake and zip. Poker faces
greet my return, the table turned.

I look down at the 10 cherubs on bicycles
on the backs of my cards on the table. They

pedal to nowhere. It's my ante. No choice.
I toss my checkered chips into the pile.

Keys to the Solar System

My wife misplaced her head
last night. This morning, brushing
her blush, her hands fluttered, *Where's my head?*
and I knew things had gone beyond

Have you seen my keys?
Bereft of pockets, she lays her keys
on any flat surface on the surface
of the Earth. I seethe, *Use your purse! Please!*

Then, *Have you seen my purse?*
She ties her purse to weather balloons
that sail over the Sea of Vapors,
crash into the Crater of Copernicus.

Have you searched the unnamed asteroids?
When she loses keys, she borrows
mine, which I am bound by wedding vows
to share. Come full moons, I make more.

By now, Dunderheads in the Solar
System carry copies of our keys.
If your ass wasn't connected to your body, Jeez!
I meant to tease, my tone, a curse.

Then, *Have you seen my ass?*
My wife's ass—finely shaped,
perfectly sized, dignified—
despite her keys, had given years of pleasure.

When

a nurse calls you

at work on a sunny Spring Saturday you hear

come immediately

drive carefully

we don't want you hurt

as well when you park

at Park West Hospital   a   mother

and   father embrace

their   teenaged son

weeping you run

into the emergency room people

waiting   for answers   stare

as if they know

why you came when

you say your name

through little holes in a window you see

an obese woman smile with yellow

teeth and lips bright red when

you feel a nurse

touch   your   hand   before the woman asks

for your insurance card

i'm nurse fellini the one who called you hear

some privacy she leads you

down a hallway clean tiled walls

              a couple cracked to pieces

        white linoleum blue

    arrows pointing

in three directions when she guides you

     into the kind of room

         you've never seen

     in a hospital before

today a cozy living

     room when nurse fellini   touches

your hand and   forearm through her white teeth

     you hear

       terrible accident when

   you lose yourself

     in eyes warm brown as the garden

           please wait

       the doctor will see you

soon when she leaves you to your

    couch comfy chair

floor lamp

      Kazhak rug with roses *fleury*

wallpaper

    a small desk with a telephone

            you knock

      your knuckles

on the chair's mahogany

      run your fingers across the couch's nap

       tight, hard as Velcro

    click the floor lamp off

  then on you turn

the Kazhak rug like

     Mohammed Ahmad Abdul Rab

        judging the loom two doctors

  walk into the cozy living room without knocking

    one in scrubs

doctor takahashi attending one

    in a wool sport coat and grateful

    dead tie

      doctor feingold neurosurgeon

loss of blood

    lack of blood

        pressure

   absent

pulse you ask

    what are you saying you hear

doctor feingold neurosurgeon

        unresponsive

    EEG reveals no

function you ask

again you hear

    doctor takahashi attending

        no respiration no

    heart

beat when you ask

        is she dead

you hear in unison   *I'm sorry*

    watching you watching them they

        depart your cozy living room

    you think of Alice's

'dee and 'dum in a race when nurse fellini

fills their empty spot you ask

    can I see her when you hear

    let me get her

        ready you taste

    something rising in your throat

that disappears when you hear

three sharp knocks

a policeman enters all

brass sparkles

blue sleeves starched by three stripes

motorcycle helmet menacing

as Achilles' tucked

under his left arm looking

straight at you

his smile gives you hope

but *I'm sorry sir*

ambulance siren

not necessary oncoming

teenager speeding he thrusts into

light pole

your hands a soul-sized manila envelope

I'm sorry sir he executes

a military about face you

see he's wearing

cop blue jodhpurs spitshined stars

reflect from knee-high black boots when

you pace your tightly-wound cocoon

you find this

                    manila   envelope

in your hands when you feel

                         lumps like   body   parts you cut

     your thumb opening the metal

clasp reach the comfy chair collapse when you tilt

                              the envelope you spill

          her wallet

                    her grandmother's wedding band

                                        an opal ring

                    her birthday gift

     nine days ago when you look

into the envelope you see

                              emptiness

you count

                    nine on your bleeding thumb when

          nurse fellini returns

                    I can take you to her

                                   now she holds

your arm to walk the hallway

          is a moving sidewalk when you approach

          swinging doors you see

your wife

through tiny windows the diameter

of truth lying

white sheet drawn to her neck

when you smell

formaldehyde and baked beans you want

to vomit when the doors click

and swish open like

two pieces of rubbed velvet when you float

into the room you stand

you notice her

freckles turned off when you look

into her open eyes

her emerald irises replaced by

pupils the size of Buffalo nickels and

a depression

pushed against her left eye socket

a child's thumbprint on a ball of Silly Putty

when you wonder whether it might be

fixed you ask

nurse fellini *is she dead* hear

I'm afraid

so and your wife confirms it

a single red bubble

        trickles from the edge of her left eye

            through a child's thumbprint

      into her strawblond hair when you think

she's crying blood you fall

              through her black pupils

    nurse fellini pulls you back

             to this morning when her straw

        berry mound rose

   with her orgasm on your tongue

seems a lifetime you float

              down under the sheet

     when nurse fellini guides

         you away when you want

     to say something to your wife when you turn

back you see a man

       in white wheel

                  her

   away

        when the doors click-swish

   open you hear

                    metal slam shut in a room

            with a drawer large enough

    to hide your life

II.

I Never Saw Him Cry

Through the layoffs
from his shop carpenter's job
where he left his sweat, his pride,
and the tops of three fingers—

through the unexpected death
of his twin, Angelo,
during heart valve surgery
on their 40th birthday,

through the embarrassment
of failing his G.E.D. exam
the same day his own son turned down
one college scholarship for another,

I never saw him cry.
The day after Lana's funeral,
at her newly dug grave,
piled high with wilting mums

and browning baby's breath,
unsettled reddish clay,
I lay down on the grass,
on my side as if beside

her in bed, digging my fingers
into her mound,
under April's blue sun.
My father walked away,

sat down in the passenger seat
of the old Buick, door open,
his black shoes planted on the asphalt,
his shoulders pulling sobs

from beneath the ground,
pouring them into his hands—
for a minute,
silencing mine.

Lana,

what if
          I had
not gone
          to work that day,
instead
          shopped with you
and
          driven the car?

Daffodils

For weeks after Lana's funeral,
my mother cooked for me,
handled death's paperwork,
opened a door—
Look outside at your garden.
Looking outward for the first time since burial
prayers, I saw daffodils blooming,
the ones that Lana and I planted
in a sunken rectangular spot last Fall,
set against the bright, new green of Spring,
Easter white and careless yellow.

Split Second To Blink

In that split second before you blinked
did you think about the blue woolen tie you bought
for my birthday resting on the passenger seat beside you
or did you think about the love we made at dawn
or me at all or the days spent on the crooked porch
of the four-room farmhouse built around the log cabin
where your grandmother—your Dawie—
was born and raised and lived until she died
where your mother was born and raised and married
where you were born and raised until your family moved to town
for high school which you pronounced "hass'cool" where
your highlight was singing "Hound Dog" at the senior talent show
did you think about your hundred-fifty-acre playground
of hills and hollows with imaginary friends and cows
in the streams that flooded banks each spring
covering the bottom lands with black silt that gave your valley
its rich Kentucky bottoms or topping green tobacco
with your daddy fastest topper in Montgomery County
or your momma worrying whether the crippled newborn calf sucked
while she fried freshly slaughtered and salted fat back on the old coal stove
or did you think about the day we combed the moldy egg crate
that your Dawie pulled from the knobless hand-made pie safe
and how the three of us swayed for hours on her creaky swing
while she mused her way through black & white you
a skinny strawblond country girl or did you think about
your family home up the hollow where your great grandmother
was born and raised and those before her and before them
to the frontier before the wars did you think about wild blackberries
we picked in the bramble and ticks we picked from each other's hair for days
or our city-boy and country-girl wedding at the ten-pewed White Oak
Christian Church or how the preacher just out of preacher school so proud
to tell a joke that he lay down *Who Am I?*

or how your city boy whispered *I Am Who Am* in your ear
just before the preacher's eyes popped open *Elvis*
or did you think about the beehive that thrived for years
in the abandoned end of the farmhouse and how we swept
decades of dead bees from our wedding bed before covering
the mattress with clean white sheets and consummating
hummed to sleep by buzzing walls did you hear the bees humming
did you remember sleeping zipped naked together in our double down bags
in our blue-domed tent did you smell the lightning strike
so close at Thunder Bay thrashing Lake Superior threatening to engulf us
did you hear the canyon gales of Cape Breton blowing
our tent away with us inside did you taste snow pelting
your freckled face skiing the frozen Straits of Mackinac
did you hear Algonquin's wolf-packs howling and
loons jeering our fear of death did you feel the love
we made in snows woods mountaintops did you
believe it turned out better or worse
or regret not finishing your degree
did you regret having no children
did you regret your turn left
did you see the Mustang
speeding chances
weren't like you
did you hear
the popping
crunching
shattering
glass or steel
did you smell
freshly topped tobacco
or taste fried fat back did
you see green-red-blue-white-

black in that split second to blink
did your Dawie reach for you from
the old farmhouse on White Oak Road
did you call her name or mine what
did you know my love?

Dyin' Blues

Delta Blues Dying,
reports *The New York Times.*
Only four men, older than Satan,
still play: one in a wheel chair
uses a butter knife to bend notes
on his hollow body Epiphone.
His piece of the Delta heard
about That Salk Man too late,
and nowadays he plays for
busloads who email his blues
far from the Mississippi's summer-
cracked silt. In Tokyo,
when they hear it,
they feel something
vibrate their bellies,
something that bends them blue.

The Minute I Found Hope

By coincidence, we each went
to visit Jane
in traction right
femur broken.

I arrived. Found her bed empty.
She's in X-Ray.
In the hallway,
lift doors opened,

to tall pain, hair gold, eyes moon blue.
She's in X-ray.
A drink? First day
with Hope, in lieu.

Elegy on a Visitation

Window open to Namesti Square,
midnight air, breezes, trash flutters.
Flakes from coal-fired electricity
reflect the sparks of the Namesti trolley,
its hourly bells pealing me to sleep
in a two-room flat, my new wife next to me.

Sparks and ashes, my first wife, Lana,
awakens me, she leads me to light
and Formica. She hands me tablet and pen.
She whispers. I write down pieces of an afterlife.

Did you find your birthday present in the car?
Did it spill onto the hood?
You loved woolen ties in winter.
Did I splatter it with blood?
Have you worn it yet for her?

Before I answer, she's through the window,
I inhale what's left of the coal-flake air.
Namesti trolleys pealing me to sleep,
sparks, flashes, rising summer suns.
My wife, Hope, awakens
to ash on the windowsill.

Elegy

I loved your taste,
freckled bananas,
a fruit devoured by my children,

Sam and Lucy,
whom you never met.
You would remember

their mother Hope,
among that group you didn't like—
too clever, witty, self-assured.

After all these years,
I still come across some
little thing—today a picture of you

and me with Hope together
by coincidence
at a Halloween Party.

Your mask, a toothy Jack O' Lantern
smile with triangle eyes.
Hers, a down turned frown, red eyes

six months before her divorce.
You stood between Hope and me—
a bridge between death and divorce,

a bridge to children
neither you nor I
believed we wanted.

Lucy is 4 "and-a-half"
she'd correct you. Her eyes
and brows are dark, like mine.

Sam, 2, a strutting motor,
is blond with blue eyes
like Hope—like you.

Their favorite flick's
The Lion King,
its theme *The Circle of Life*

by Elton John and Tim Rice. Still alive,
Tim and Elton and Sam and Lucy and Hope
and I. But you,

undone
when a left turn, hurried,
didn't beat a speeding Mustang.

You didn't need the siren.
Last week, I found an empty
envelope with your name—

Lana. By now,
when Disney's lions and kings
surround Sam and Lucy,

they twirl around my fingers
and sing *The Circle of Life,*
inventing lyrics, rhyme, and beat,

oblivious to copyrights or Elton John
or births by accident.
They sing it endlessly, and loud.

Sanguine Noce

The Pittsburgh steel mills spew red dust,
smell it, touch it in daylight,
see it at night,
the orange glow behind the next hill
from Upland Street in the Homewood neighborhood.
The red-brick shotgun houses
shoot out Italian immigrants,
Black migrants, Slavs, Poles
in eight-hour shifts
for the Frankstown Road street car,
transfer down to the Monongahela River,
down to the mills
from the red-brick row houses
where my father was born,
where I was born,
where on Christmas Eve, the table laden
with calamari and lasagna and—
oh! only at Christmas and weddings—
sanguine noce.

A Roman would pronounce with delicacy
song-WEEN-uh NO-chay, twirl
spaghetti in black sauce on his fork.
My grandfather, a crude Pugliese dirt farmer,
shouted it *ZUNG-wuh-NACH*
and kept chickens in the backyard,
chickens in the cellar of this row house in Homewood,
a block from the Frankstown Road streetcar line.

On Christmas Eve, my grandmother Madalena yells,
Eh! Vito! Gallina! A sanguine noce!
And I follow him
to the cellar, sit on the steps
while he chases a hen from the backyard,
through the cellar door, around the boiler,
both of them squawking Italian,
he grabs the hapless hen
by its neck and legs
so it can't scratch and peck,
carries it to the washtub,
where I hear him snap its neck
with one calloused hand,
a sound like a knuckle cracking,
with a serrated butcher's knife,
saw the dead hen's head from its body—
splintering tendons, bones—
carefully spills spouting blood
into a metal cup, and, almost full, hands it to me.
Uppa, Tommy, uppa. Nonna, she's a-wait.

I cradle the cup upstairs
to my grandmother, standing over the stove,
simmering the chocolate sauce,
watch her pour the fresh blood into the pot,
add a handful of *pinolas*, stir
soft, white nuggets into the sweet, black sauce.
I run back down to the cellar
to watch Vito pluck and gut the chicken.
Those old-country dagos used every part—
intestines, organs, brains, claws, eyes—
nothing could be wasted.

I tell my wife this story every Christmas
as we prepare our free-range turkey from Whole Foods,
its neck and liver stuffed inside.
My wife doesn't like the story,
beneath her Savannah heritage,
which predates the Civil War
and contact with living or bleeding chickens.
At the end of my tale,
without fail, I turn my back to her,
zip the turkey neck into my trousers,
hung in all its glandular glory,
and I swing around to face her,
Honey, how about it?
Never works—she makes me throw it away,
as if somehow soiled by my joke,
another lost opportunity for *sanguine noce.*

III.

My Little Heart Attack

went by so fast
it didn't stop my singing
or my dancing with my children—
twirling Sam and Lucy, their long hair flying
until ventricular tachycardia
at two too many beats per measure
sat me down to rest my chest.
I took my tricky heart to Dr. Takahachi.
He said, "Let me palpate
your thorax. Breathe. Yes. Copasetic."
Someone else called nine one one

when myocardial infarction
hiding in my warty arteries
started stallions galloping across my sternum
and the EMS responded, pounded
KY Jelly into my ribs,
convulsed me repeatedly
with portable defibrillator paddles
while I danced and twirled.
"Again! Again!"
they called like Sam and Lucy
denying it's time for bed.

Robins and Orioles

Flying northeast, robins and orioles
feast by the hundreds in the yards

below, chirping fury of spent birds,
gluttons for the glowing garnet holly berries.

My children stare, keep vigil for half an hour
while I read *New British Poetry* in my peaceful chair.

My wife takes the children out for an hour
or so. The first thump I hear

against the back door
barely cocks my ear.

At the second pop,
my eyes jump

from Sujata Bhatt.
The third splat

motivates me. My guess—
a bird full speed whacking glass.

At the back door,
one dead robin, an oriole quivers on the deck floor,

wing shattered, eyes black and blinking,
thorax thumping.

The orange & gold feeding frenzy continues
sans these two azoic cousins

and me. What to do? Lana would weep
and nurse the oriole back to flight. Hope would weep

and shy away. The children,
due home soon,

would demand inspection,
then dissection.

I go to the garage for the shovel.
The azalea leaves shuffle—

as the robin and oriole fly through—swish-swish,
two thumps on the dark, sweet mulch.

The Inventor

I. Inspiration

It's February, we're skiing cross-country
through the Straits of Mackinac,
icy crystals sting her naked cheeks.

She stops to point her tips to shore.
I have to pee,
she shouts into the wind.

First, her bindings, then
her Gore-tex ski pants, next
her Thinsulite, skin tight,

at last her panties,
and a sapling strong enough to grasp
while squatting,

her clothes around her ankles
below. I bend, blow breath
on my cupped hands

and palm her chilly cheeks. Afterwards,
we tug and struggle, layer by layer,
finally, clip her boots into her skis.

I feel an urge. I can't resist
my turn to pee.
Look. Two zips. I'm done.

She smacks me with one pole
plants the other, glides away
like wind across Lake Huron's ice.

II. Invention

Spring thaw comes late to Lakeshore Drive,
the rain against the Hancock Tower,
the lightning flash as I walk home.

Forget the sketches, I go right
to a flexible sheet of plastic,
cut and shape with heat,

then cover every edge
with soft, felt gaskets, add
a foot of ½ -inch Tygon tubing.

Finish just in time
—her 30th birthday gift—
I call it the Stand Tall Urination Device.

My birthday message reads,
I would stoop forever,
unclip, re-clip, your bindings—Love.

That winter, she's testing it on skis.
I tinker with her suggestions,
streamlining, tightening, adding a belt.

By Spring, she starts to wear it around the house.
By June, I notice all her newer slacks
have zippered fronts.

III. Evolution

My wife, the Kellogg School of Business
M.B.A., deserves credit
for all that follows.

With her "vision" training, she files
a patent claim, invents a product name,
creates campaigns for *Redbook*, *Lifetime*, WebMD.

By God, she lands a spot on Oprah.
We build a cash cow up in Michigan
—Detroit—

manufacture Women of the World! Stand Up®
in our basement,
then in an empty drive-shaft plant.

Across the U.S., women
nowadays, prefer their powder rooms
with urinals—

My wife? Oh. A good question.
Today, she stands almost alone,
our marriage packed in ice

after the Kimberly-Clark buyout.
She shipped me to the Bangkok plant
as head of product development

to design implantable versions
that generate friction—
orgasms for women who select

our recommended elective
surgery. My wife got F.D.A. approval
for tomorrow's kinds of love.

Dense Nodular Opacity

Doctor's letter—
results of your routine physical,
routine chest X-ray,
read twice to discover
which lung violates routine.
The doctor, circumspect, encloses directive—
Piedmont Hospital Radiology. *ASAP.*

That January Saturday clouds
our New Year, darkens
sleep 'til Monday,
when you go for deeper probes.
The radiologist says, *2 days for results. Call your doctor.*

Google-meisters, each of us
searches for secrets
of dense nodular opacities.
You have no symptoms, no risk factors.
Never smoked nor lived with a smoker.
Not a coal miner. Nor a solvent-factory worker.
20 percent of women who succumb
never smoked, you discover.
When lung cancer shows itself,
I discover, it's too late—
load revolver, bite barrel, pull trigger.
You discover it may sprout from:
Ovary. Uterus. Brain. Blood. Bone.

We wait. We weep, embracing.
If it weren't for the children, you say, *I wouldn't care.*
How am I going to raise Sam and Lucy alone? I think.
I don't want to be one of those women people talk about, you say.
This can't happen to me, again. I think.

Two days later, still no answer.
You say, *A CAT scan will be the next step.*
Then, a biopsy.
I think, *Without your income, we'll lose the house.*
You say, *Surgery. Followed by radiation.*
If I'm lucky, no chemo.

When you're bedridden, wasting,
I will sit by your side day and night,
hold your hand, clean your breathing tube,
wipe your shit.
Morphine at the end will help
you discover religion again,
visits from angels flying around the room.

Sam will ask, *Why is momma so skinny?*
Lucy will say, *Momma isn't pretty anymore.*
Sam will ask, *Why is momma crying?*
We'll get to watch more TV, Lucy will say, *and eat more candy.*

The Plan:
A one-night-only viewing,
no funeral. Cremation. Urn.
Sam will ask, *When will we see momma again?*
Lucy will ask, *Are these little white chips mom's bones?*

On the third day, we rise again
from sleeplessness. The doctor calls.
Your dense nodular opacity
is not a tumor, but calcified tissue
from, best guess, some childhood affliction
you cannot on your life recall.
We drink a bottle of *Beaujolais Nouveau,*
reassured that, by the odds,
I will be the first to die.

Sam and Abraham

8 million gods of Shinto mythology
selected two of their own
to order chaos from the formless void.
Izanagi, strong as a willow,
and his sister Izanami, delicate as air,
stirred with a jeweled spear
the sea until it thickened to mud,
until drops falling from its tip
formed Onogoro-jima, the first island of Japan,
and they walked on Onogoro, indulged
their delight on delightful Onogoro,
delight that begat,
as in all creation myths,
complications.

8 million gods—that's a lot to a 6-year-old,
even to one steeped in myth,
and his first question to me—
Could 8 million Japanese gods
defeat our one God?
Sam stratifies his world
—who or what is stronger, smarter, better—
in the way of boys and men since Adam.
Could an American tank defeat Polyphemus?
Could Hercules defeat a vampire?
Could Zeus defeat pollution?
No. Yes. Probably. I don't know.

I prepare for *Why?*
Instead, his blue eyes widen:
All the gods from mythology—
they are pieces of our one God!
I hear a box click shut in his mind,
a sound that cinches my throat like a noose.
I taste blood,
grieve over the loss of 8 million gods.

Smoking Volcano Tops

As we stumble toward a new Earth,
I'm going to miss all but the first steps.

I will be dead before warming's full heat
cracks ice caps like a too long boiled egg.

My children might not live to see
the meltdown, and for that I'm glad—

since humans rose up
from the mud of Australopithecines,

like them, I've hoped to leave behind
a better world to my children, but

failing, I would like to live
long enough to witness:

Britannia ruled *by* waves,
Lady Liberty up to her breasts

like some drowning Ozymandias
imploring Give me your *puddled* masses,

New York's Empire State Building,
bathed to its navel—the Washington

Monument—its pyramidal pediment
peaking over wind-blown amber waves.

I want to witness it all,
want answers to my questions:

Will Micronesia become
Millimicronesia? What about Indonesia?

More *pelago* than *archi*?
Vanuatu, Borneo, Dominica?

What's left of them—smoking volcano tops?
I want to know what happens

to skinny nations like Chile.
And poor Holland!

I want to know which cities could bid
on the Winter Olympics of 2278.

The *New York Times* reports that air as warm
last blanketed Earth 150,000 years ago.

Back then, *Homo* was newly *sapiens*.
The last hominids who weathered such climate

hunted large mammals with sticks, gathered
nuts, berries, yet to discover wild grains.

Tools or wheels, neither invented.
The human diaspora from the Rift Valley

hardly begun. Farming? 140,000 years away.
Carbon footprints? Only small wood fires.

I was not among them then.
I will not be among them again.

A Grip on the Blues

On a standard diatonic harmonica, the reed for hole #2 may be bent on the draw from its natural note to three lower notes, in half-steps, both going down or up the scale, to create either distinct notes or a continuum of sound. Several other holes may be bent to a lesser extent. This technique was first used by Mississippi Delta harmonica players in the early 20th Century, thus creating the bluesy sound of what's commonly called the cross-harp position.

The Poet Chooses His Drug

SSRI is Selective Seratonin Reuptake Inhibitor, the clinical name for the class of anti-depressants that includes Prozac®, Zoloft®, Serzone®, and others.

PDR is *Physician's Desk Reference*, which contains listings of all drugs approved by the Federal Drug Administration.

Her Constellations

Ptolemy, Hevelius, Tycho Brahe are early astronomers.

Andromeda, Lyra, Camelopardalis, Draco, Cygnus, Canis Venetici, Pegasus, Boötes, Coma Berenices, Lynx, Corona Borealis, Triangulum, Cancer—all are heavenly objects: Constellations, galaxies, or stars.

Games of Chance

The HER-2/*neu* oncogene is a marker in a breast tumor that increases the chance of metastasis exponentially. It is considered a marker for vastly decreased prognosis, as survival rates for those with this oncogene decline by 75% or more.

Cyclades—islands off the coast of Greece that include Santorini, Myknonos, Ios, Milos, Serifos, Hydra, and others.

Keys to the Solar System

The Sea of Vapors and the Crater of Copernicus are features on Earth's moon.

Elegy on a Visitation

Namesti Square is in Prague, Czech Republic, where soft coal is burned for electricity, and the coal flakes often "snow" upon the city. The better grades of coal are sold abroad.

My Little Heart Attack

Ventricular tachycardia is an irregular heartbeat that sometimes presages a heart attack.

Myocardial infarction is the clinical term for heart attack.

The Inventor

The Straits of Mackinac separate the upper and lower peninsulas of Michigan, and at this point, Lake Michigan empties into Lake Huron. In winter, the shallows of the straits and the shore waters often freeze, allowing cross-country skiers a flat, though windy, wonderland several miles long.

Sam and Abraham

Stanza 1 summarizes the main details of the Shinto creation myth.

In Gratitude

To April Ossmann for shaping this manuscript.

To Cathy Smith Bowers, Steven Cramer, Alan Michael Parker, and Rebecca McClanahan for shaping these poems. To Ron Rash, Major Jackson, Michael Kobre, Richard Chess, and Fred Leebron for sharpening my craft and my mind.

To my colleagues, too numerous to name, who have critiqued early drafts of these poems, especially Susan Meyers, Pat Riviere Seel, Terri Wolfe, and the Queens Poets.

To Kevin Watson for his design of these pages and for his faith in my poetic sensibilities.

To the memory of my wife Lana S. Lombardo, whose untimely death, far too young, bent my life.

And to my wife Catherine Hope Dlugozima for her unbending love, inspiration, and courage.

Tom Lombardo is a poet, essayist, and freelance medical writer who lives in Midtown Atlanta. Tom's poems have appeared in journals in the U.S., the U.K., Canada, and India (translated to Hindi and Mayalayam), including *Southern Poetry Review, Ambit, Subtropics, Hampden-Sydney Poetry Review, Aethlon: The Journal of Sports Literature, Atlanta Review, New York Quarterly, Chrysalis Reader, Pravasi Duyina, Thanal Online, Ars Medica,* and others. His nonfiction has been nominated for a Pushcart Prize, Best of the Small Press, 2009. He was editor of *After Shocks: The Poetry of Recovery for Life Shattering Events,* an anthology featuring 152 poems by 115 poets from 15 nations. Tom runs the Poetry of Recovery blog at www.poetryofrecovery.blogspot.com. His criticism has been published in *New Letters, North Carolina Literary Review,* and *South Carolina Review.* He earned a B.S. from Carnegie-Mellon University, an M.S. from Ohio University, and an M.F.A. from Queens University of Charlotte. Tom is poetry series editor for Press 53, which is based in Winston-Salem, North Carolina.

CPSIA information can be obtained at www.ICGtesting.com
Printed in the USA
LVOW13s0817130813

347618LV00003B/156/P